W9-DGE-849

Life, Death, and Christian Hope

Daneen Georgy Warner

Paulist Press
New York/Mahwah, NJ

Night Prayer (see Introduction, note 3) is taken from Lawrence Lovasik, SVD, *Saint Joseph Book of Prayers for Children* (Totowa, NJ: Catholic Book Publishing Company, 2000). Reprinted with permission.

Cover design by Sharyn Banks
Book design by Lynn Else

Library of Congress Cataloging-in-Publication Data

Warner, Daneen Georgy.
   Life, death, and Christian hope / Daneen Georgy Warner.
      p. cm.
   Includes bibliographical references.
   ISBN 978-0-8091-4596-6 (alk. paper)
   1. Death—Religious aspects—Christianity. 2. Jesus Christ.
3. Laments. I. Title.
   BT825.W314 2009
   236'.1—dc22

                                                        2009002659

Published by Paulist Press
997 Macarthur Boulevard
Mahwah, New Jersey 07430

www.paulistpress.com

Printed and bound in the United States of America

Contents

"Do you not know that all of us who have been baptized into Christ Jesus were baptized into his death? Therefore, we have been buried with him by baptism into death, so that, just as Christ was raised from the dead by the glory of the Father, so we too might walk in the newness of life. For if we have been united with him in a death like his, we will certainly be united with him in a resurrection like his." (Rom 6:3–5)

Dedication
For my three sons, Erik, Brandon, and Adam,
who encourage me to live my gift of life
with a hopeful, vulnerable heart.

This book is meant for all my companions in the Christian tradition. The reflection questions at the end of each chapter are guidelines to encourage your own thinking on how the meaning of your baptism is lived out in your daily life. Whether you read the book at home, on retreat, or in a church study group, I encourage you to keep a journal or notebook on how your personal struggles and joys define your life journey in relation to the ideas offered in my book. I am very interested in your thoughts on my themes and reflections as well as information on different settings in which you found my book helpful. You are welcome to e-mail me your thoughts and insights at lifeanddeathmatter@gmail.com.

Acknowledgments

This book is possible only because I decided to listen to God and follow God's path for me. Most of my family and friends have survived the difficult change in my life journey from big corporate paycheck and perks to the joy and peace of living God's way through service to others as a chaplain. In this regard, I am grateful to my sons, Erik, Brandon, and Adam, my husband, Michael, and my sisters, Joanne and Dianne, who each helped me in their own important yet unique ways. Also, I am grateful to Angie, Bill SJ, Cecily, Denise, Grace, Kay, Jan, Mark, Maggie, Marie, and Mary Ann, who walked with me as dear friends and supporters, even when I wondered whether I would ever see God's light at the end of a very long tunnel. In addition, I am deeply thankful for my parents, Mary and John Georgy, who both entered eternal life while I was discerning God's will for me. My mom and dad prepared me for my new path by introducing me to God's love from the moment of my birth. I have felt their constant presence as well as that of others within the Communion of Saints. Some of these friends are Doris, Patti, Mary, Mary O', Tony, Thomas, Teilhard, Paul, Jane Frances, Clare, Francis (2), Catherine, Therese, and Teresa (2).

There are many more friends, relatives, acquaintances, and colleagues who have contributed directly or indirectly to this book. I am particularly grateful to Rev. Donna Claycomb, who extended her hospitality to me as I discerned God's will that I attend Duke Divinity School. Due to her support, I now see the many fruits of my years at such a wonderful place where God's love crosses many human boundaries. Also, I extend special thanks to my friend and thesis advisor Professor Allen Verhey, who guided and encouraged me to plunge into my own depths with God beside me, as I reflected on the meaning of hope within death from many different perspectives. I also deeply appreciate the Duke Institute on Care at the End of Life (ICEOL), which offered me a scholarship for my ThM studies, and its director, Dr. Richard Payne, who read my thesis and encouraged me to seek publication.

My sincere appreciation extends as well to Rev. Lawrence Boadt, CSP, at Paulist Press who accepted my manuscript for publication. In addition, I am deeply indebted to my editors Paul McMahon and Nancy de Flon for their careful reading of my manuscript and insightful comments that helped transform it into a practical reflection on the hope of our "daily dying."

Introduction

Now I lay me down to sleep,
I pray the Lord my soul to keep.
If I should die before I wake,
I pray the Lord my soul to take.
Amen [1]

How many generations of children have said this prayer on their knees at bedside each night? What kind of parents would teach a prayer about death to small children? And why? I can only speculate from my experience of having been taught the prayer and having taught it to my three sons. First, the prayer is a simple truth about life: life will end but the Lord keeps your soul. This is faith. Second, going to sleep is practicing dying every night. However, the Lord is present and protective even when alone and in the dark. This is hope. Third, because this prayer is usually said within the context of the Communion of Saints as our "cloud of witnesses" (Heb 12:1–2), the Lord's care and protection extend through others both living and dead. This is love. Thus, the three theological virtues seem to be the essence of this prayer that prepares the child for the night no matter what happens, even death.[2]

In today's Western culture, however, death appears to have been extracted out of Christian faithfulness and thrown into a human-contrived cesspool of pornographic objectification. As a result, the culture takes on the role of death's master as it teases, taunts, and attempts to control death. For instance, many parents dare not mention death unless it happens as "killing," "zapping," or "eliminating" another in a "fun" controlled environment such as a video game or cartoon. The message is loud and clear: "You can control death, and if the bad guys happen to zap you, then you will eliminate them the next time." One children's bedtime prayer of contemporary vintage mentions nothing about the possibility of death and the Lord as the safe keeper of souls.[3] What has changed and why? What does our aversion to discussing death and teaching the way of Christ's Cross tell us about our culture and our life as Christians today?[4] What exactly is our theology of death? Does it challenge our Christian practices for a "life well-lived" in keeping with Christ as our model? Or does our working theology of death "march to the beat of a 'cultural' drummer"? That is to say, does our working theology of death display a trust in science and technology to fend off our mortal end through an idolatrous trust and hope? If yes, how does this impact our lives as Christians? What happens to our lives if our faith and hope depend on human efforts and its technology instead of God? What happens when the hope in technology fails and when human efforts fail or disappoint? Does faith in technology turn to despair? And if we despair, can we still love and be loved?

This book attempts to redirect these questions through the lens of Christian hope. It proposes the following scenario: Because Christians accept life as a good gift from God, death is always difficult. However, the secular culture's influence misleads Christians to deny the truth of the human condition—a tortuous life journey that encounters pain and suffering as well as joy and happiness. As a result, Christians resist death rather than accept death in light of Christ's Cross and Resurrection. Also, in this denial, Christians ignore their need for lament, an important practice along life's journey. Without lament, Christians tend to cling to faith and hope in human efforts instead of faith and hope in God, that is, divine hope.[5] As a result when human hope and faith fail, despondency and despair frequently result.

This book also recasts the preceding gloomy scenario and, in doing so, challenges Christians to reframe death and dying in three ways. First, Christians are called to acknowledge the truth about the human condition. Having done so, Christians are free to accept lament as an important Christian practice for moving from a dependency on hope in human efforts to hope in God. Second, with lament Christians are better able to accept dying and death in response to the good news of holy scriptures, baptism, and the Eucharist. The good news is that "Christ has died, Christ is risen, Christ will come again"—the mystery of faith and source of Christian hope.[6] This hope through God's grace moves Christians to love others within an eschatological community that transcends both time and place. Third, Christians transform faith communities in light of the good news so that love flourishes in daily dying to self through living out the Beatitudes for others. As a result, the preparation of daily dying forms Christians to accept dying and death not as the worst evil to resist in every way but rather as the final stage of a lifelong journey with Christ into eternal life. "Death, while still retaining its dreadful and enigmatic powers, becomes, through faith, an opening to the divine presence....Death while still a terrible reality, is an enemy God has taken into his own life, through Christ, and overcome in him.... We can move through death and resurrection into God's life."[7] Thus dying is not even the final stage, but rather a lifelong journey of modeling the life of Christ!

In developing these three ways for reframing dying and death, we will proceed through five steps. First, we examine the Western culture's deceitful perspective of the human condition as a lived experience in opposition to Christ's truth. Second, we explore the essential role of lament in acknowledging the bad news about the human condition so that human hope is capable of transforming into hope in God (divine hope) as a paradoxical "joyful lament." Lament is thereby viewed through scripture and the sacraments of baptism and Eucharist. In addition, practical examples will demonstrate joyful lament versus "joyless lament." Third, we examine the good news of divine hope for the lifelong journey of dying and death demonstrated in scripture, baptism, and Eucharist. Fourth, in order better to understand the church's role in Christian faith formation concerning dying and death as a lifelong journey with Christ, we explore how living the good news from a pastoral ministry context is realized "in the trenches" by considering some of the key observations offered by clergy and church members from a variety of Christian traditions.[8] Finally and fifth, we consider a few recommendations concerning Christian formation for dying and death as a lifelong journey with Christ.

Questions for Reflection

1. Considering your life journey since childhood, how has your prayer life changed with your understanding of life and death in relation to faith, hope, and love?

2. Describe your awareness of the influences of the secular culture on your habits and practices of daily living.

3. How does your personal life story enhance and diminish your willingness to flourish in light of God's good news?

CHAPTER ONE

Cultural Deceit versus the Christian Vision

Unmasking Cultural Deceit

What is the lived reality concerning dying and death in Western secular culture today? Philippe Ariès appropriately defines the present as the era of "wild death,"[1] a concept that has been explained as "not only a technological death, but a hidden, dirty death, one that is shunned, feared, and denied."[2] A more "tame death"[3] that is considered "the oldest death there is" prevailed until the eighteenth century when "the combination of cultural and religious changes, and the rise of scientific medicine, brought it to an end."[4] According to Daniel Callahan, Ariès views tame death of earlier centuries as "tolerable and familiar, affirmative of the bonds of community and social solidarity, expected with certainty and accepted without crippling fear."[5] On the other hand, modernity's wild death is marked by "undue fear and uncertainty, by the presence of medical powers not quite in our mastery, by a course of decline that may leave us isolated and degraded. It is wild because it is alien from, and outside of, the cycle of life, because modern technology makes its course highly uncertain, and because it seems removed from a full, fitting presence in the life of the community."[6]

Tolstoy's *The Death of Ivan Ilyich* describes the entry of wild death in the nineteenth century through the dying of Ivan and the lie he is forced to go along with:

> Ivan Ilyich suffered most of all from the lie, the lie, for some reason, everyone accepted: that he was not dying but was simply ill, that if he stayed calm and underwent treatment he could expect good results. Yet he knew that regardless of what was done, all he could expect was more agonizing suffering and death. And he was tortured by this lie....A lie that was bound to degrade the awesome, solemn act of his dying to the level of social calls...he came within a hairbreadth of shouting: "Stop your lying! You and I know

that I'm dying, so at least stop lying!" But he never had the courage to do it. He saw that the awesome terrifying act of his dying had been degraded by those about him to the level of chance unpleasantness...that it had been degraded to the very "propriety" to which he had devoted his entire life. He saw that no one pitied him because no one even cared to understand his situation. Gerasim [pantry boy] was the only one who understood him and pitied him...Gerasim was the only one who did not lie.[7]

What change promulgated such a drastic movement from tame death, dying and death intricately woven into the stream of life, to wild death, dying and death brutally cut off from care and compassion through denial and lies? One possible answer can be found in the writings of German philosopher Immanuel Kant. According to Kant, the "Enlightened" way of living—the practices and thinking of the Enlightenment—would "release men and women from their self-incurred tutelage and free them to know and especially to master their world."[8]

This mastery abandons traditional ways of understanding human life and directly focuses on what has become the greatest evil, namely, mortality or human finitude. As a consequence, dying and death become captives of the realm of science and are reduced to the ultimate numbers game.

According to Joel Shuman, in Enlightenment thought "any way of life that suggests that the final end of humankind is not found in the quantification and finally in the mastery of the world is rejected a priori."[9]

Enlightenment thought prevails today and continues to look to science and technology to control nature and in doing so to conquer human finitude in what Gerald McKenny calls the "Baconian project."[10] Additionally, René Descartes' famous axiom *cogito ergo sum*—"I think, therefore, I am"—gives rise to a dualism concerning the mind and body of the human being. Shuman explains, "Descartes suggested, proceeding from a methodology of universal doubt, that the mind, the *res cogitans*, was an immaterial thing interior to and completely distinct from the body, the *res extensa*."[11] For Descartes, the body is purely a machine limited by physical laws while the mind is free and unconstrained. Christian doctrine, on the other hand, opposes any dualist sense that the mind and soul exist separate from the body. Geoffrey Wainwright notes, "If our bodies are not us, then we are not responsible in and for them; and that irresponsibility may assume the character either of license or, indeed, of withdrawal. The same phenomenon occurred in the gnosticism of the second century."[12] As Alastair MacIntyre observes, "when the body is understood as material and passive, it can readily be seen as an object for or an exemplification of the results of scientific research."[13]

It is in medicine and its clinical research that the frightening effects of the "Baconian project" become evident. Two of these effects are of particular interest to us. First, death defeats the means of the clinical "project," namely, the clinical treatment regime/research protocol/clinical guidelines. In other words, the "project" is the apotheosis with death as its enemy. Lately, even doctors admit that what scares them most about the healthcare system is "being the patient."[14] A story in *Time* magazine reported that "scientific knowledge improves, but the care doesn't keep up; it is easier to gather gigabytes of information than to acquire the judgment to apply it wisely."[15] This statement raises interesting questions about care, judgment, and applied wisdom—things that the pantry boy Gerasim seems to comprehend better than not only Ivan Ilyich's doctors but possibly even doctors in the twenty-first century.

The second effect concerns medicine as an institutional force in a capitalist system dependent upon economic expansion fed by the masses' "unappeasable appetite not only for goods, but for new experiences and personal fulfillment."[16] The economics of medicine follows that of consumer capitalism. Medical techniques produce financially reimbursable results that provide economic expansion. However, medical techniques are isolated activities disconnected from the full story and social relationships of the person. Shuman observes that "[medicine] has operated to help alienate modern persons from their bodies, from one another, and hence from meaningful, community-based ways of living and dying, all the while masking its coercive alienating tendencies under the guise of final truth about human life and death."[17] This alienation includes a clinical system that operates independent of a true moral and religious framework. In doing so, the "Baconian project" also bolsters the ideals of self-determination, individual rights, and entitlement.[18] Because people have no true moral compass, they have a cultural expectation and a perceived right to access all medical technology in an effort to eliminate their mortality and secure their inner fulfillment. As a result, most people, including many Christians, place their faith and hope in medicine. In doing so, they harbor a false sense of security concerning their mortality. They then become paralyzed with a fear of dying with the onset of any perceived healthcare crisis. Because medicine typically focuses on techniques for bodily control, the needs of a sick and/or dying person as fully embodied and relational are ignored, leading to further suffering and trauma. Thus, a "good" death in the secular world is a cessation of bodily function that minimizes pain and suffering for the dying patient. Unfortunately, the isolation of a dying person whose only hope is medicine's false pretense (Ivan Ilyich's lie) of last-minute immortality frequently leads to despair.

Allen Verhey provides a helpful reflection and important question concerning this situation:

> The irony, of course, is that science does not tell us what to do with the great power it gives. It does not tell us what ends to seek or what limits to observe. It cannot tell us how to use these great powers without violating the human material upon which they are used. At the end of the story, even as we continue to tell it, we know better. Human progress cannot be reduced to scientific progress. Knowing a patient cannot be reduced to scientific knowing. Indeed, the scientific "view," if the complaints are to be credited, can distort our vision and blind us to persons and to the body as "me." But if religion and philosophy have been left behind as "theological" and "metaphysical" ways of knowing, then where shall we look for guidance?[19]

I suggest that Gerasim has a lesson or two about life, dying, and death, especially considering that Ivan seems to have lived his life completely out of touch with his own existential reality of mortality. Yet it is only through Gerasim that Ivan is able to accept the truth of his dying and impending death while finding the company, comfort, and compassion for which his very soul yearns. Gerasim's lesson is one of compassionate care given simply because "'We all have to die someday, so why shouldn't I help you?' By this he meant that he did not find his work a burden because he was doing it for a dying man, and he hoped that someone would do the same for him when his time came."[20]

In contrast to Ivan's lifelong denial of mortality, Nathan Coulter in Wendell Berry's novel *Hannah Coulter* lives a life as a farmer in a small Kentucky community where relationship to one another and the land is a way of life. The seasons of the year with the seasons of life flow as naturally as the river with water that paradoxically wanders with direction through his community of Port William. When Nathan starts feeling unwell, his dear wife Hannah observes,

> For a good while after he got sick, he thought he would just work it off the way he always had, he would get well. And then the truth came to him, and he faced it. After that, he was loitering, putting us off, giving himself a chance to be captured by his death before he could be captured by the doctors and the hospitals and the treatments and the tests and the rest of it. When he consented to go to the doctor he was only consenting for the rest of us to be told what he already knew. He was dying....He wanted to die at home. He didn't want to be going someplace all the time for

the sake of a hopeless hope. He wanted to die as himself out of his own life. He didn't want his death to be the end of a technological process.[21]

The Corrective Vision: Death through a Christian Lens

Both Ivan and Nathan seem to yearn for the truth about the finitude of life's journey. Both may remind us of the earlier concept of Ariès' tame death, and both invite consideration of the earlier practice of the age-old tradition of *ars moriendi*.[22] Is it possible that the Christian community could correct their vision of dying and death if they were to reclaim the practice of *ars moriendi*? The question is beyond the scope of this book, but I do want to raise two points concerning *ars moriendi* instructive for reimagining life in view of the truth of dying and death.

Based on Daniel Callahan's view of the key features of tame death in the *ars moriendi* tradition, I think "familiar simplicity" and "public character" are worthy considerations, especially in light of Christ's Cross.[23] First, earlier in our history death was familiar to every age because mortality rates were higher and people frequently died at young ages. Interestingly, although most people today in the West live longer, death is still a fact for every person. The big difference seems to be the denial of death in today's culture. However, if Christians accept the truth of Christ's Cross as reality, then would it be possible to stop resisting death and become familiar with its presence as a routine part of daily life? Could the following advice offered in the *Imitation of Christ*, a classic of fifteenth-century *ars moriendi* literature, also find meaning today for Christians? "See how in the Cross all things consist, and in dying on it all things depend. There is no other way to life and to true inner peace, than the way of the Cross and of daily self-denial. Go where you will, seek what you will; you will find no higher way above nor safer way below than the road of the Holy Cross."[24]

The second worthy consideration of tame death in *ars moriendi* is its public character. In earlier centuries, nothing was more important than to have a dying person surrounded by family, friends, and community members fully immersed in the daily routines of living. The reason for this is not only to provide compassionate care but also to provide communal unity between the living and the dying and even the dead in the Communion of Saints. As Ariès puts it,

> It was not only an individual who was disappearing, but society itself that had been wounded and that had to be healed....The rites in the bedroom or those of the oldest liturgy express the conviction that the life of

this man is not an individual destiny but a link in an unbroken chain, the biological continuation of a family or a line that begins with Adam and includes the whole human race.... Thus, death was not a personal drama but an ordeal for the community....It could not be a solitary adventure but had to be a public phenomenon involving the whole community.[25]

What difference would it make today if daily dying of one another then continues with dying persons united as one community of the past, present, and future through Christ's Cross and Resurrection? Is not this same sense of dying in community both "familiar" and "public" in every church that represents Christ's Cross and Resurrection through the Real Presence at the Eucharistic Table?

Even if these two considerations would be enough to initiate a reimagining of dying and death today, there is still the important reminder that life in general and dying and death in particular take on an entirely different meaning from the secular world when Jesus Christ is the focus. Death is the end of life on earth. However, the obedience of Jesus to the Father turns the curse of death into a new path *through* dying and death *to* eternal life for all those who have faith.[26] Pope John Paul II acknowledged that "death as such is not a good; it is rather an evil, the deprivation of the good of life, and as such an affront to the dignity of the human person."[27] Death is not good, but Christians believe that Christ removes the sting of death through his suffering, death, and Resurrection. In this regard, the Spiritual Exercises of St. Ignatius focus on a theology of Christ's Cross that has three distinctive marks:

> It reflects fully the reality of suffering that leads to death; it is related to the whole of the Paschal Mystery (from the incarnation to the resurrection); and it stands as a symbol of hope. The cross reveals a resurrection which is not only a future hope, but a reality occurring in history as people take others down from the crosses of suffering. As such, the cross is central to a Christian eschatology that not only points to a future, but draws human beings together in solidarity as they put themselves at the service of the promised hope which the resurrection reveals.[28]

Thus, the Christian death has a positive meaning due to Christ. "For to me, living is Christ and dying is gain" (Phil 1:21). As a result, death is both bad and good news. The good news is that through baptism Christians have already "died with Christ sacramentally, in order to live a new life; and if we die in Christ's grace, physical death completes this 'dying with Christ' and so completes our incorporation into him in his redeeming act."[29] The good news continues in the Eucharist, through which

Christ provides his body and blood as the source of life to overcome death. "As often as you eat this bread and drink the cup, you proclaim the death of the Lord until he comes" (1 Cor 11:26). Cardinal Avery Dulles calls the Eucharist "the sacrament of death swallowed up in Christ's victory" and shared among all who are willing to partake in Christ's life.[30] Theologian Dorothee Sölle actually defines a Christian as "a person for whom death is behind him."[31] Thus, a "good" death for a Christian acknowledges human mortality and the limited time to fulfill our baptismal promises of faith in Christ, hope of eternal life, and love of God and one another. If this sounds familiar, it is. The good news of the "good" death is Christ's Cross reflected in both Ariès' tame death and the earlier practices of the *ars moriendi* tradition. We will later examine some scriptural and sacramental perspectives concerning this good news after we tend to the "bad news."

But there is also room for suffering in this picture. Everyone who is born also dies. Every day is one day closer to our final day on earth. The Christian existentialist Søren Kierkegaard believed that despair is sin and the torment of despair is an inability to die. This sin of despair is the opposite of faith in God. Kierkegaard thought that everyone experiences this despair except true Christians who don't dwell in the unity of the individual but rather in the unity of relationship with God.[32] The roots of much of Kierkegaard's existentialist thinking on death can be traced as far back as St. Augustine. For example, in his *Confessions* Augustine expresses his deepest feeling about death as he reflects on the death of his close friend in Thagaste. He says:

> Black grief closed over my heart and wherever I looked I saw only death....Everything I had shared with my friend turned into hideous anguish without him. If I bade [my soul], "Trust in God," it rightly disobeyed me, for the man it had held so dear and lost was more real and more lovable than the fantasy in which it was bidden to trust....I should have lifted it up to you, Lord, to be healed, but I was neither willing nor able to do so, especially because when I thought about you, you did not seem to be anything solid or firm. For what I thought of was not you at all; an empty fantasy and my own error were my god.[33]

Today's secular culture seems to uphold Augustine's "empty fantasy" about death. In the words of the General Convention of the Episcopal Church, it "conspires against acknowledging [death's] inevitability. Death in our secular society typically provokes fear and denial, rather than contemplation and reflection. And so our society deals with death by evasions and lies."[34]

And if that isn't enough, in some form or fashion we, as well as our loved ones, will suffer concerning our dying and death. When Christ suffers, so also does his Father suffer. When we suffer, Christ suffers and our Father suffers. However, if Christians are expected to model Christ in suffering, dying, and death along the Way of the Cross, then Christians must also model Christ in crying out in protest against this dire predicament. There may be neither a resignation to the lies of the culture nor silence in self-isolation. But rather Christians are called to join Jesus in Gethsemane and on the Cross. If Christ, who went to "a death he freely accepted," cried out in a prayer of lament on the Cross—Psalm 22, "My God, my God, why have you forsaken me?"—then Christians too may cry out loud to God in their sufferings.

Questions for Reflection

1. Considering your own life journey, recall your experiences in observing tame death and wild death. Describe any differences or similarities between these two experiences. What emotional, psychological, physical, and spiritual responses did you have in observing tame death and wild death?

2. How does the present clinical healthcare system's technological approach affect you, your family, friends, church, and community? How does the present system affect how people live and die? Imagine that you could change today three things about the present system. What would you change and how would your changes impact the way people live and die?

3. How might Gerasim's compassionate care and Nathan Coulter's seasons of life relate to your views on death and dying?

4. Imagine that you are dying and must choose today between permanent life on earth or eternal unity with God. What would be your considerations in making your choice?

5. What is your theology of suffering? How does it affect the way you live your life and your relationships with others?

6. Reflect on the three marks of the theology of Christ's Cross. How does the Cross transform suffering into hope? What examples of this transformation can you recall from your life experiences thus far?

CHAPTER TWO

The Importance of Lament

Reclaiming Lament

T hus far, I have attempted to challenge the illusive lies of a Western culture trapped in Enlightenment thinking and its wild death. In addition, we have revisited Ariès' notion of tame death with its familiarity and communal approach to life preparation for dying and death, and then viewed tame death through Jesus Christ's death and Resurrection that bears the good news that through suffering comes life.

Before examining, through the lens of scripture and the sacraments of baptism and Eucharist, the good news of a lifelong journey modeling Christ in dying and death, however, I want to contend that Christians must first acknowledge the suffering attendant upon dying and death. In doing so, Christians are called to cry out in lament as they willingly open themselves to trust in the Lord's love—a necessity for rejecting the culture's seduction to resist death. If Christ had to acknowledge the dread of pain and suffering before he could resign himself to his Father's will, then Christians must do the same. Thus, lament is the next essential step if Christians are to reframe dying and death in light of Christ as the way, the truth, and the life (John 14:6).

The important role of lament in the reframing of dying and death will be considered in four steps. First, I will define lament and then describe it as the transitional practice between a hope in human efforts and a hope in God. Once grounded in hope in God, Christians are then better able to accept daily dying and death in light of Christ's death and Resurrection. As a consequence, Christians live within the divine paradox of daily dying within Christ's "new life"—that is, a Christian life of joyful lament. Second, I will use examples from the Old and New Testaments to demonstrate the movement of lament from human to divine hope. Third, I reflect on the relationship between lament and the sacraments of baptism and Eucharist. Finally, in order to provide a practical grounding for the essential role of lament in reframing dying and death, I look at some practical examples of joyless lament and joyful lament, returning again to Ivan Ilyich and Nathan Coulter.

There is no denying the history of human pathos and the unquestionable need for humans to voice their complaints, anger, and bitter frustration concerning the brokenness of God's creation. If we did not do so we would be oblivious to reality. *Where* the human voice focuses these complaints, however, makes all the difference in whether or not the complaint is a fruitful endeavor or consummate frustration. In this regard, the psalms are a great gift because they are poetic expressions of the deepest feelings expressed in prayer originating with God's Chosen People Israel. In addition, the psalms cover every human emotion from utter joy to absolute lament. It is the lament psalms that have particular appeal for our purposes.

A lament is a complaint or a cry to the Lord for delivery from a distressing situation. Sometimes lament is a penitential cry. In many situations, however, the lament is a cry of a sufferer who has no sense of wrongdoing. Sometimes the lament is an individual cry; in other cases, it is a communal complaint. In every case, lament exposes the raw emotion of the pain and frustration with the human condition.

The basic structure of the lament psalm is an address to God; complaints about the pain and suffering experienced; a confession of faith in God's power; a petition for God to act; and thanksgiving for God's care. While all five elements are not always found in every lament, the progression from the lamenter's earthly situation to recognition of God's presence in the human condition always seems to be present. It is in this progression of awareness from human to divine that hope in God is found. Allen Verhey identifies within this progression a shift where "suffering looks heavenward.... Lament, too, gives the suffering voice....The sufferer is helped to find words that hold hope for a saving reversal and that nurture the reconstruction of a faithful identity, a faithful direction."[1] Thus, it seems that hope in human efforts can shift to hope in God once lament expresses the anguish of passing through the fire of pain and suffering. Dominican theologian Edward Schillebeeckx says, "Christian hope, in its most radical form, is born precisely amid the experiences of negativity, darkness, and injustice in which human beings cry out in protest: 'This cannot go on!' In the indignation, lament, and active resistance to which these 'negative contrast experiences' give rise, the eyes of faith can detect the power of the Spirit of God at work on behalf of the future of humankind and the cosmos."[2] Within this shift, lament in a kenotic[3] action seems to empty a Christian's "broken vessel" of dependency on hope in human efforts and refill it with hope in God.

Psalm 13 demonstrates this kenosis through a progression of awareness and shift from dependency on human hope to divine hope:

> [1]How long, O Lord? Will you forget me
> forever?
> How long will you hide your face
> from me?
> [2]How long must I bear pain in my soul,
> and have sorrow in my heart all day long?
> How long shall my enemy be
> exalted over me?
> [3]Consider and answer me, O Lord my God!
> Give light to my eyes, or I will sleep
> the sleep of death,
> [4]and my enemy will say, "I have prevailed";
> my foes will rejoice because I am shaken.
> [5]But I trusted in your steadfast love;
> my heart shall rejoice in your salvation.
> [6]I will sing to the Lord,
> because he has dealt bountifully with me.
> (Ps 13)

The psalmist begins with a strong protest addressed to God (v. 1–2). The intensity of this protest seems to be emphasized with the use of "how long" four times in two verses. In verse 3 the psalmist further shifts toward God through an urgent petition with a specific response. The psalmist then proceeds in verse 4 to provide God a rationale for his or her petition. The psalmist continues to shift toward hope in God in verse 5 by expressing trust in God's love. Finally, verse 6 expresses thanksgiving through song "because [God] has dealt bountifully with me." It is interesting to note that the great Christian mystic Bernard of Clairvaux has specifically readdressed part of this prayer to Christ: "O good Jesus, give light to my eyes, lest I sleep the sleep of death and my enemy says, 'I have prevailed against him.'"

The Movement of Lament in Scripture

The Book of Lamentations provides a good example of human complaint that stops short of lament—a cry of anguish that looks from the present to the past and *not* toward God's good future: "How lonely sits the city that once was full of people!… Jerusalem remembers, in the days of her affliction and wandering, all the precious things that were hers in days of old.…And her prophets obtain no vision from the Lord" (Lam 1:1, 7; 2:9). This is sometimes referred to as a dirge.[4] In contrast, the psalms of lament display the kenotic or "emptying" action through which human hope is transformed into divine hope.

In Psalm 13, the lament empties the lamenter of present and past anguish so that he or she feels confident in the Lord's help. Claus Westermann explains: "Only by this clinging to God has the suppliant a future. Only then does he come out of his lament and look forward to the possibility of his lament turning into praise. But this is more than just anticipation. The suppliant promises that the salvation he now entreats will determine his future...."[5] Thus, the psalmist abandons hope in human powers for hope in God's good future.

The New Testament offers instances of dependency on hope in human powers with all its uncertainty instead of hearts open to divine possibilities. One example is that of the Pharisees and Sadducees, who, despite the uncertain times for the Jews under Roman rule, seem to place all their hope in their own certainty concerning law and procedures. As a result, they block any possibility of recognizing the hope in God through the good news of Jesus Christ. Another example is Pilate, who lives in fear of the Roman regime and the repercussions if the Jewish people stage an uprising. Pilate places his hope in the Romans and in himself. He realizes that there are false witnesses at Jesus' trial and that Jesus is handed over out of envy (John 18:28—19:16). Consequently, Pilate is blocked from seeing Christ's divinity and yields to those calling for Jesus' death.

Lament has no space for those who nourish hope in human powers and its future of uncertainty. But we can also look to three New Testament events that nicely highlight lament and the shift from trust in human powers to trust in God. First, in the Jewish tradition of that time people in mourning did not leave the house for seven days except to visit the tomb of the deceased to grieve.[6] Thus, with the death of Lazarus, Martha and Mary would have been lamenting for four days before Jesus arrived in Bethany. Martha rushes out to greet him, openly expresses her grief concerning her deceased brother, and within her exchange with Jesus confirms her belief in his divinity. "Yes Lord, I believe that you are the Messiah, the Son of God, the one coming into the world" (John 11:27).

The second New Testament event is that of the suffering Christ who is destined to bear the Cross. Christ laments this suffering. "And going a little farther, he threw himself on the ground and prayed, 'My Father, if it is possible, let this cup pass from me, yet not what I want but what you want.'...Again he went away for the second time and prayed, 'My Father, if this cannot pass unless I drink it, your will be done'" (Matt 26:39, 42). Christ laments his suffering as distance from God and affirms so through his words of Psalm 22:1 while on the Cross. Thus, the very human Jesus, knowing with certainty what is about to take place, surrenders to the will of his Father. Having emptied himself to the Father, Jesus shifts to absolute trust in his Father.[7] Christopher Vogt identifies three qualities of Christ's hope in Gethsemane: "First, it relies for comfort on the assurance of God's constant presence in the midst of suffering. Second, it moves Jesus to continued action as God's witness. Third, it includes an eschatological dimension or an expectation that God's presence is more powerful than death and endures beyond it."[8] These same qualities of hope or trust in God are present to faithful Christians in the sacraments and serve to support a Christian life of daily dying to self. This observation calls for further commentary later.

The third New Testament event involves Cleopas and another disciple who are walking to Emmaus from Jerusalem on the day of Christ's Resurrection. While there is no definitive scholarship to confirm their discussion "about all these things that had happened" (Luke 24:14), their grief concerning Christ's death and their suspicion that reports of Christ's Resurrection are "an idle tale" (v. 11) support the likelihood that they would have lamented. The uncertainty of hope in human power must have been overwhelming. However, Jesus the stranger begins opening their eyes to the reasons why it was "necessary that the Messiah should suffer these things and then enter into his glory" (v. 26). Then Jesus offers hospitality as the catalyst for transforming hope in human power to hope in God: "when he was at table with them, he took bread, blessed and broke it, and gave it to them. Then their eyes were opened, and they recognized him" (v. 30–31). While their hearts had already been burning within them as Jesus revealed the scripture along the road, "he had been made known to them in the breaking of the bread" (v. 35). Does the transformation of trust in human power to hope in God continue within each Christian's personal Emmaus walk and through the sacraments?

The Emmaus story points us directly to the significance of the Eucharist. We will now continue by relating the essential purpose of lament in reframing dying and death to the theological significance of the sacraments. In particular, baptism and the Eucharist provide for lament during the transforming shift from human to divine hope in preparation for Christians taking up their crosses of daily dying within the Lord's grander, eschatological kingdom.

Questions for Reflection

1. Read through the psalms in Holy Scripture in order to find your own favorite lament psalm. Reflect on this psalm. Why is this lament psalm meaningful to you and your life story? What are your feelings before, during, and after reciting this psalm?

2. Compose your own short psalm of lament using most of the five elements that comprise the basic structure of a lament psalm.

3. What role does protesting to God about your human condition play in your routine prayer life?

4. The Book of Lamentations provides an example of a cry of anguish that looks despairingly to the past instead of hopefully to God's good future. What present day situation(s) or event(s) focus more on what was, rather than what could be through hope in God's good future? Consider the tension between hope in God and the perceived need for human control.

5. Recall a situation in your life in which you seemed more dependent upon human powers than upon divine possibilities. What was this experience like for you?

6. Recall a situation in your life that demonstrated lament shifting from hope in human powers to hope in God. What was this experience like for you? How does this experience compare with your experience in Question 5?

CHAPTER THREE

From Joyless Lament to Joyful Lament

Lament, Baptism, and the Eucharist

The Christian paradox concerning hope is apparent in the sacraments of baptism and Eucharist. While they are rooted in the reality of life on earth and all that is of the earth,[1] these sacraments have every intention of moving Christians toward the Lord's Heavenly Banquet. What an amazing, paradoxical balance with the fulcrum being Christ's Paschal Mystery! Living with this paradox, however, calls for lament as Christians struggle between the often deceitful power of human hope, which is riddled with uncertainty, and the faithfulness required with hope in God.

In baptism, lament occurs during the formation process of the catechumenate and is apparent in three images that have existed since the early Church. The first image is the "Sign of the Cross," a very ancient prayer practice that can also be considered a sign of lament. According to St. Basil in the fourth century, "we learned the sign from the time of the apostles and that it was administered in baptisms. Some scholars interpret St. Paul's saying that he bears the marks of Christ on his body (Gal 6:17) as his referring to the Sign of the Cross."[2] Not only is this sign made upon the initiated one's forehead with blessed oil at baptism; it also identifies the person as a follower of Christ. However, practicing the Sign of the Cross as a mark of discipleship certainly would cause the initiated person to lament for two reasons. First, the Sign of the Cross means that the new Christian has agreed to shed his or her former identity and take on a new life in Christ. As Paul says, "So if any one is in Christ, there is a new creature; everything old has passed away; see, everything has become new!" (2 Cor 5:17). What a leap of faith it takes to walk away from the familiarity of one's present life and take on a totally new self with new goals, values, and aspirations based on the model of a man named Jesus who lived thousands of years ago! In the case of an infant baptism, the parents must certainly have reason to lament, "signing" over the identity of their child to a "perfect" stranger who died thousands of years ago as a common criminal via a brutal crucifixion.

The second reason a newly initiated Christian might pause to lament the Sign of the Cross is its significance as a pledge that Christians accept the life of Christ, including the way of Christ's Cross with all its sacrifice, unselfish love for others, pain, suffering, and even death. Paul proclaims, "Who will separate us from Christ? Will hardship, or distress, or persecution, or famine, or nakedness, or peril or sword? As it is written, 'For your sake we are being killed all day long; we are accounted as sheep to be slaughtered.' No, in all these things we are more than conquerors through him who loved us" (Rom 8:35–37). Certainly reason for lament prior to making the Sign of the Cross!

The second image concerns purification from sin. That is, during formation the catechumen laments his or her sinfulness. Peter exhorts, "Repent and be baptized every one of you in the name of Jesus Christ so that your sins may be forgiven; and you will receive the gift of the Holy Spirit….Save yourself from this corrupt generation" (Acts 2:38, 40).

The third image is the descent into the waters of baptism—an intimidating event, especially in the early Church that practiced full immersion. This immersion is a "physical mimesis of burial"[3]— another good reason for initiating lament. However, the focus of the lament shifts when the newly baptized Christian emerges from the water clothed in new life that holds the qualities of Christ's hope—a divine hope.[4] "Do you not know that all of us who have been baptized into Christ Jesus were baptized into his death? Therefore, we have been buried with him by baptism into death, so that, just as Christ was raised from the dead by the glory of the Father, so we too might walk in the newness of life. For if we have been united with him in a death like his, we will certainly be united with him in a resurrection like his" (Rom 6:3–5). In baptism, divine hope fosters daily dying to self as Christians "put on Christ" and become living witnesses to God's good future.

The Eucharist is "the source and summit of the Christian life."[5] Also, the Eucharist continues to carry the radical theological claim of baptism concerning the Paschal Mystery: "Christ is present, the rule of God is very near, in fact the gifts given in the water bath and in the holy meal obliterate the conditions that keep us separated and alienated. We are reconciled to God and to neighbor. The communion is a foretaste of glory divine and a foreshadowing of the New Jerusalem."[6] While this is indeed good news, there is still a challenging struggle to reconcile the obvious disparity "between this reality that is offered and what our social body is capable of receiving."[7] On the other hand, when Christians come together to celebrate the eucharistic liturgy, there is a sense of human pathos not only in recognizing personal and corporate shortcomings, but also in realizing that the Lord's kingdom is not yet fully realized. Saliers explains,

Until the day of the Lord, we gather in that *deep pathos of memory* of God with us. Still deeper is the *pathos of hoping* for God's promises yet to be fulfilled. Without remembering that creation is a gift, without remembering that our lives are gifts, without remembering that the whole history of God with the earth points toward the liberation from bondage and death made real in Jesus, we can never begin to grasp the hope that is offered to us in the symbols, words, and the ritual actions of the Christian assembly.[8]

The Roman Catholic Mass or Lord's Supper consists of the Liturgy of the Word and the Liturgy of the Eucharist. Following the introductory rite of welcome, in the penitential rite we express our sorrow for our individual and corporate sinfulness. This lament begins not so much as a confession to God of human sinfulness but rather as Christian awareness of the faith journey away from sin and evil and toward God's good grace and divine life. With Christ's presence on this journey, we begin, with the confession of faith and priest's absolution—"May almighty God have mercy on us, forgive us our sins, and bring us to everlasting life. Amen"—to turn to trust in God.

The Liturgy of the Word—a reading from the Hebrew Scriptures (or, in Easter time, the Acts of the Apostles), a Responsorial Psalm, a New Testament reading, and the good news of the Gospel—offers the interweaving of lament and hope as it puts before us God's intervention in human history and God's continued faithfulness and care through all our adversities and despite our struggles with sinfulness.

At the consecration "the power of the words and action of Christ, and the power of the Holy Spirit, make sacramentally present under the species of bread and wine Christ's body and blood, his sacrifice offered on the cross once for all."[9] It is in this eschatological moment that the common body and earthly elements meet the divine. Once this happens there is no looking back to cling to baseless hope in earthly things. For this reason, the great sacramental gift of Christ's presence is followed by thanksgiving and praise to the Father in union with the entire Communion of Saints—one body of Christ that spans all time and place. The lament becomes speechless prayer of one's entire mind, body, and soul that embraces all the qualities of Christ's divine hope. With hope in God, Christians are ready to partake in Christ's body and blood as one body of Christ. Finally, the priest's blessing sends forth Christians with a renewed sense of trust in God and the joyful lament of their daily dying in service to others through living the Gospel.

Thus far, I have attempted to show that lament is an important practice in the movement of hope in human power to hope in God – an essential requirement for the practice of daily dying and a "good" death. We now move to the final step of providing a few practical examples of the lived reality of lament both as joyless lament and joyful lament.

Living the Paradox of Joyful Lament

When the human cry protesting the emptiness of consumerism never seeks a hearing from God, then the search for human powers in which to hope wanders from one fruitless substitute to another. A compelling example is to be found in the character of Stein—his name means "stone"—in Peter De Vries' *The Blood of the Lamb*.[10] Stein is the embodiment of cynicism, sarcasm, and despair. He seems absolutely hopeless—a bleak, black hole of a man devoid of not only hope in God but also hope in humans. Don Wanderhope describes his attitude as "one of assertive hopelessness."[11] As for God, Stein says, "God is a word banging around in the human nervous system. He exists as much as Santa Claus....Prove to me that there is a God and I will really begin to despair."[12] He also believes that "life is a fatal disease."[13] However, Stein's dismantling of the Beatitudes truly demonstrates the depth of his despair.[14] He also puts his own cynical interpretation on Christ's words in Luke 23:29 with this chilling display of utter despair: "'Blessed are the wombs that never bare, and the paps that never suck,' Stein said. 'Could this be the Son of Man preparing himself for those final words against the black sky, the last, cosmic turn of the wheel of agony, the hoax at last seen through: My God, my God, why hast thou forsaken me?'"[15]

On the other hand, Wanderhope moves through lament and is an example of joyful lament. Even when in doubt, he holds onto a glimmer of hope in responding to Stein's despairing remarks: "You mean you're not *sure*? Why, man, that's great! For the rest of us, who like to hug that little doubt we so desperately need today—what faith was to folk of another time—the ray of hope. Oh, how grateful we are for that uncertainty!"[16] Wanderhope shares lament with Mrs. Schwartz.[17] He shares his own "vignettes of human collapse"[18] where hope in the human meets hope in the divine. Wanderhope collapses in a "mist of tears" while pleading his cause before God in front of the shrine to St. Jude, patron of lost causes and hopeless cases.[19]

Wanderhope begins seeing the divine in his daughter's wounds—her stigmata. He recognizes that he stands on holy ground as Carol is close to death.[20] Wanderhope whispers the following benediction during their last moment alone: "The Lord bless thee, and keep thee: The Lord make his face shine upon thee, and be gracious unto thee: The Lord lift up his countenance upon thee, and give thee peace."[21] Then touching each of his daughter's stigmata, he says "Oh, my lamb."[22] After flinging the cake at the crucified Christ, he hears the divine voice saying "'Suffer the little children to come unto me...for of such is the kingdom of heaven.'"[23] Finally, recognizing that his grief over Carol will never disappear, he understands the truth in his "dying" through the Beatitude "Blessed are they that comfort, for they too have mourned."[24]

One of the most moving examples of the transformation of lament is found in Nicholas Wolterstorff's *Lament for a Son*.[25] I know of nothing written in recent history that captures the depth of emotion and love expressed in Wolterstorff's lament. An entire essay could be written detailing Wolterstorff's movement from the dashing of human hope to the embracing of hope in God through the five elements of a lament. I will attempt to capture six highlights of his experience.

First, the intensity of Wolterstorff's grief surfaces when he asks, "Now he's gone, lost, ripped loose from love; and the ache of loss sinks down, and down, deep down into my soul, deep beyond all telling. How deep do souls go?"[26] Second, his sense of loss of certainty and human hope seems to be captured in his questioning whether or not something demonic lurks in the world responsible for what happened to his son.[27] Also, he doesn't believe in the world's promises anymore. He says, "What the world gives, I still accept. But what it promises, I no longer reach for."[28]

Third, Wolterstorff seems to move his lament toward the divine when he questions what he will do with his "God-forgiven regrets" and allows his wounds to "sharpen the vision and intensify the hope for the Great Day coming when we can all throw ourselves into each other's arms and say, 'I'm sorry.'"[29] In addition, the author continues to open his lament to God in exploring Psalm 42 where "lament and trust are in tension, like wood and string in bow."[30] Fourth, when Wolterstorff begins acknowledging the great mystery of a God who shares human suffering, he begins to see his image in God. "Do we also mirror God in suffering?"[31] Fifth, Wolterstorff moves toward hope in God when reflecting on the Beatitude "Blessed are those who mourn, for they shall be comforted." He says, "The mourners are those who have caught a glimpse of God's new day, who ache with all their being for that day's coming, and who break out into tears when confronted with its absence."[32] Finally, Wolterstorff "struggles to live the reality of Christ's death and rising,"[33] accepting the wounds of his son's death and beginning to rise from his suffering love. Thus, Wolterstorff's acceptance of divine hope seems to help him accept his "dying" so he may continue living for others who also need his love.

A final contrast between joyless lament and joyful lament involves Ivan Ilyich and Nathan Coulter once again. Ivan Ilych lives within the lie of his human hope for his entire life. He plays it safe, looking out for himself with hope in his own selfish principles of living. Death has no part in Ivan Ilych's life. He shares the same thoughts as his colleagues: "Well, isn't that something—he's dead, but I'm not."[34] That is, until he is faced with a life-threatening illness. Suddenly, he must depend on others to take care of him. He now becomes the object of the very deceit and lies that he routinely dished out to others. Human hope runs out: "He was in a constant state of despair. In the depth of his heart he knew he was dying, but not only was he unaccustomed to such an idea, he simply could not grasp it, could not grasp it at all."[35] Ivan Ilych still tries diversions and escapes, especially his work. But his condition worsens and even his own dying is out of his control. Ivan Ilych's joyless lament is three days in a dark hole of constant screaming, "uttering screams with that 'O' sound."[36] However, emerging from that dark hole he understands love for the first time—his crucial acceptance of hope in God just moments before his death.

In contrast, Nathan Coulter lives and dies in a farm community reasonably free of deceit and lies. "Kindness kept us alive. It made us think of each other....Love is what carries you, for it is always there, most in the dark....We had made it past hard changes, and all of us changed but we were together."[37] Having accepted his dying, Nathan tells his wife in response to her question about what he plans on doing, "Dear Hannah, I'm going to live right on. Dying is none of my business. Dying will have to take care of itself."[38] Nathan has no interest in "hopeless hope"[39] because he has been living with hope in God for a long time—a joyful lament!

Questions for Reflection

1. Reflect upon your baptism in the context of lament and its three images discussed in this chapter. What insights about your hope in God does this perspective offer you?

2. Reread Saliers' explanation about viewing the human pathos in the light of being a gift. Next consider the many gifts in your life during a typical day. Make a list of each of God's gifts that you have been blessed with in your life over the past twenty-four hours.

3. Can you think of present day examples of "spiritual" bonding in the consumer culture that provides a constant bombardment of fleeting possibilities for hope in our earthly existence? What (if any) cultural entrapments have misled you into holding onto false hope(s)?

4. Write your own short narrative about a person(s) in your life experience whose attitude reflects Stein's "assertive hopelessness." What was it

like for you to be around this person? Did you learn anything about yourself as a result of this experience? If yes, what?

5. Wanderhope views uncertainty as a gift that holds a ray of hope within his joyful lament. What do you think about uncertainty as a gift? Recount an experience(s) in your life when uncertainty influenced the outcome or your decision. How would you describe your sense of hope and lament in this experience(s)?

6. Reread the description of Wolterstorff's movement from the dashing of human hope to the embracing of hope in God through the five elements of lament. Recalling your own life experience, write a short narrative that traces the same movement of hope using the five elements of lament.

CHAPTER FOUR

Living Love: The Logic of the Cross

Thus far, I have attempted not only to unmask the effects of the culture's lies concerning dying and death, but also to argue for the importance of acknowledging the presence of suffering through the practice of lament. Lament acts as a bridge between complete dependency on hope in human or earthly things and utter dependency on hope in God. Crossing that bridge is an occasion for joyful lament. Once they have accepted the practice of lament, I believe, Christians are better able to appreciate the good news about dying and death in the light of Christ's death and Resurrection. However, this new appreciation only comes through daily dying to self and love of others—something that is almost impossible to maintain without hope in God. This section addresses this good news as found in scripture, baptism, and the Eucharist.

Because God's good future has not yet arrived, lament is an ongoing practice that continues throughout life; pain and suffering are as common an occurrence as joy and happiness. In addition, the grief of past trials continues as an important part of our life stories. Once we have embraced hope in God, however, daily dying becomes a transforming experience through the same self-emptying (*kenosis*) found in Jesus. In this kenotic state Jesus becomes his Father's fully revealed presence in the world. This presence is love as his Father is perfect love for all of creation. With eyes focused through faith on hope in God, then Christians become Christlike. According to theologian Jürgen Moltmann, "the key to nurturing Christian hope (what I call hope in God) is the development of a willingness to give one's whole self to the kingdom of God as revealed in Jesus Christ."[1] In doing so, Christians in love turn continually outward to others while continually dying daily to self. Through this reaching out, the Christian focus is connection to others. Christ's love becomes our love in a complete unity so that "it is no longer I who live, but Christ who lives in me" (Gal 2:20). In this regard, Augustine says, "You are the Body of Christ; this is to say, in you and through you the method and the work of the incarnation must go forward. You are to be taken, you are to be consecrated, broken and distributed, that you may become the means of grace and vehicles of eternal charity."[2]

But what does it mean to be "vehicles of eternal charity"? It means that we become "carriers of care" so others might live! In other words, the saving action of God puts Christians into Christ's death and Resurrection (Rom 6:3–4; Col 2:12) and they become Christlike. In becoming so, Christians share their love of others through self-giving acts of charity. Thus, "dying to self" becomes a joyful lament and the good news about dying and death. A corollary effect of this good news is that bodily death loses its sting in contrast to the typical death under the secular culture's influence (1 Cor 15: 55–56). Because Christians experience their *real* death and then rebirth as children of God at baptism, Christians are no longer alienated from God and death's sting dissipates.

What revelation and support system does God provide as we strive to live the good news? To answer this question, let us focus on three areas: first, the Hebrew Scriptures as the source of God's revelation to God's people; second, the model and further revelation of Jesus and the disciples in the New Testament; and finally the sacraments of baptism and Eucharist.

The Lord's good news begins with Genesis, the first book of the Hebrew Scriptures. God, who is love, made humankind in his image. Thus, human beings have been created to image God in love from the very beginning. "So God created humankind in his image, in the image of God he created them; male and female he created them" (Gen 1:27). When humans turned inward to focus on self-love before love of God and others, they become enslaved to and oppressors of the world and one another. But God's love for humankind never changes, and God responds to our cries for help. God not only led the Chosen People out of slavery but also enrolled them in his forty-year "wilderness school."[3] Wilderness schools build character by teaching the skills to survive under highly challenging conditions. Lutheran pastor Daniel Erlander Christianizes the concept of wilderness school and summarizes its lessons as follows:

We own nothing. All is God's. All is gift.

God gives enough for all to be shared by all.

Hoarding causes rot. It stinks.

Work is helping God distribute manna, the gift God promises to all.

God gives rest so humans can practice full time what life is all about....Friendship with God, Friendship with others, Friendship with nature.[4]

In his wilderness school, God taught the good news of a people who image God by being a people of love who are willing to practice daily dying to self so others may live.

Despite the setbacks we experience after the initial school, God's love prevails. God made a covenant with the Chosen People in the wilderness, and that covenant is continued and fulfilled in the incarnation of God's Son Jesus, our Savior. The image of the vine and the branches occurs frequently in the Hebrew Scriptures to refer to God's faithfulness to his covenant and his ever-present help to us when we fail. "In days to come Jacob shall take root, Israel shall blossom and put forth shoots, and fill the whole world with fruit" (Isa 27:6). "Restore us, O God of hosts; let your face shine, that we may be saved. You brought a vine out of Egypt; you drove out the nations and planted it. You cleared the ground for it; it took deep root and filled the land....Why then have you broken down its walls, so that all who pass along the way pluck its fruit?...Turn again, O God of hosts; look down from heaven, and see; have regard for this vine..." (Ps 80:7–9, 14). In Psalm 81, God reminds his people again about the lessons taught in wilderness school:

> ...I am the Lord your God,
> who brought you up out of the land of
> Egypt.

Open your mouth wide and I will fill it.
"But my people did not listen to my
   voice;
Israel would not submit to me.
So I gave them over to their stubborn
   hearts,
to follow their own counsels.
O that my people would listen to me,
that Israel would walk in my ways!...
I would feed you with the finest of the
   wheat,
and with honey from the rock I would
   satisfy you." (Ps 81:10–13, 16)

In the New Testament, God's good news is personally delivered through his Son, Jesus Christ. God's love is so perfect that he is willing to risk his own Son to the wayward and cunning ways of humankind. Even in his death, however, the good news continues as Christ destroys death through his Resurrection. Henri Nouwen describes the Resurrection as "the expression of God's faithfulness to Jesus and all God's children. Through the Resurrection, God has said to Jesus, 'You are indeed my beloved Son and my love is everlasting,' and to us God has said, 'You indeed are my beloved children and my love is everlasting.'"[5] Love is truly stronger than death and God's love prevails again in providing divine hope for his people who have faith, love, and practice the lessons of God's original wilderness school.

Jesus is the fulfillment of God's covenant. Jesus continues the teaching of God's original wilderness school, and he perfects those teachings through his emphasis on love and his own modeling of those teachings through his selfless love. We will look at four examples of Jesus' approach to teaching.

First, Jesus teaches with parables

> how to live as a manna society, a restored Israel, a community of the reign of God (Luke 5: 27—6:49)....His parables rattle his listeners by portraying something so valuable in their midst that it would be foolish not to drop everything to receive it. What was this precious pearl, the lost sheep, the lost coin, the beckoning home, the tree home for birds? The precious thing was nothing less than a new society, a renewed Israel open to all...a realm of God's extravagant grace, mercy, forgiveness, and compassion... a place where those labeled unworthy or impure are received unconditionally....A world of abundant manna shared by all....a reality worth dropping all other commitments to joyfully receive.[6]

Second, Jesus not only proclaims but also personally demonstrates the good news by living as a herald of God's reign through love and compassion for others. Jesus' own life is "living love." God sends his Son to love more than anything else. The authorities were so intimidated by Jesus' refusal to restrict his love that they conspired to kill him. As liberation theologian Virgilio Elizondo explains it, Jesus lived the "Galilee principle": God taking on human flesh "in the midst of contaminated, corrupt believers. God chooses 'what is low and despised in the world' (1 Cor 1:28). God's word is revealed among the impure people of the borderland: 'Search and you will see that no prophet is to rise from Galilee'" (John 7:52).[7] Because the poor and abandoned are closer to understanding the good news, God's Son chooses to be like them and not like the authorities, who are intimidated by vulnerability. Love is vulnerability because self diminishes through love of others. Christ the Galilean lives the Beatitudes that he teaches on the Sermon on the Mount (Matt 5). Through this teaching, Christ also calls his followers to become the "salt of the earth" and "light of the world" (Matt 5: 13–16). These followers, however, are the outcasts whom the world rejects and yet are the "salt of the earth"—a precious substance that keeps the earth alive in so many ways. Lutheran theologian Dietrich Bonhoeffer commented that the disciples are "not only directed toward the Kingdom of God, but also reminded of their mission on earth. As those bound only to Jesus, they are directed to the earth, whose salt they are. By calling not himself, but his disciples the salt of the earth, Jesus assigns to them an activity on the earth. He draws them into his own work."[8] Bonhoeffer emphasizes the way Jesus delegates his life of "living love" through the Beatitudes to all his disciples until the end of time. Once again the good news becomes the only news worthy of our attention and action!

Third, Jesus understands the challenges of the human condition. So he preaches the parable of the vine and the branches. Jesus knows his scriptures; thus he not only builds on the imagery of Psalm 80—"You brought a vine out of Egypt..."— and on Isaiah 27, but he also appropriates an image from the everyday world in which his listeners lived. Jesus is the vine and his disciples are the branches. While the human condition can distract a person from acting upon the good news, Jesus offers reassurance that by staying connected as a branch to his vine all will be well. "Abide in me, as I abide in you. Just as a branch cannot bear fruit by itself unless it abides in the vine, neither can you unless you abide in me" (John 15:4). In John's Gospel, this is Jesus' final parable before his last days on the way to his Cross. Significantly, his disciples are also called to walk the way of Christ's Cross through daily dying to self and then final death. Only through connection to Jesus, however, does this challenging journey make sense and become a labor of love.

Connection to Jesus means connection to others as well. As Nouwen observes, "the great gift hidden in our dying is the gift of unity with all people."[9] The unity is the foundation of the good news because daily dying is done not in isolation but rather in connection with others. At the same time, even bodily death transcends isolation due to our connection with Christ as members of the body of Christ—the Heavenly Banquet that gathers the Communion of Saints, though not yet fully realized.

Fourth, Jesus "walks the talk." Because Jesus loves humankind as only God can love, Jesus not only proclaims the word, but also dies the death of a criminal when his only crime is love for others. Jesus truly makes the human cry of lament his own cry. For those who have faith and hope in God, however, connection to Jesus also means sharing in his Resurrection—a joyful yes to eternal life within God's kingdom. How do we know this? Jesus makes such a promise when he prays to his Father

> ...that they may all be one. As you, Father, are in me and I am in you, may they also be in us so that the world will believe that you have sent me. The glory that you have given me I have given them, so that they may be one, as we are one, I in them and you in me, that they may become completely one so that the world may know that you have sent me and have loved them even as you have

loved me. Father, I desire that those also, whom you have given me, may be with me where I am, to see my glory, which you have given me because you loved me before the foundation of the world. (John 17: 21–24)

For the support par excellence for the journey of dying and death, we must look to the sacraments of baptism and Holy Eucharist. Baptism effects a transformation into a new person by grafting that person onto Christ. As Orthodox theologian John Zizioulas writes, "Thanks to Christ man can henceforth himself 'subsist,' can affirm his existence as personal not on the basis of the immutable laws of nature, but on the basis of a relationship with God which is identified with what Christ in freedom and love possesses as Son of God with the Father....This adoption of man by God is the essence of baptism."[10] Thus, baptism seals the connection with Christ so that the baptized person becomes one with the body of Christ. Paul proclaims that in baptism the newly initiated enters into communion with Christ's death, is buried with Christ and rises with Christ as well. "Do you not know that all of us who have been baptized into Christ Jesus were baptized into his death? We were buried therefore with him by baptism into death, so that as Christ was raised from the dead by the glory of the Father, we too might walk in newness of life" (Rom 6:3–4; Col 2:12). However, having "put on Christ" also means becoming Christ through daily dying to self while giving love and service to others – the good news.

Because of our human condition, our journey toward becoming Christlike takes a lifetime. Thus, along this journey our patient, merciful, and compassionate Lord feeds us with the bread of new life—Christ himself in the Holy Eucharist.

The Liturgy of the Eucharist brings together the truth of the pathos of human history with the ethos of hope in God's promises, not yet fully realized. The ultimate expression of this truth is the Real Presence of Jesus Christ in the Eucharist, through which Christians find both the strength to live the good news and the path to eternal life. Christ addresses the challenge of the truth of his Real Presence to his disciples by assuring them, "Very truly, I tell you, unless you eat the flesh of the Son of Man and drink his blood, you have no life in you. Those who eat my flesh and drink my blood have eternal life....Those who eat my flesh and drink my blood abide in me, and I in them" (John 6:53–54, 56). Thus, Christ unfolds two critical truths about the essential purpose of his Real Presence in the Eucharist. First, Christ in the Real Presence provides us the *strength* to be a Christlike presence living the good news in a world that disdains truth. Second, it is through partaking in Christ's Real Presence that Christians journey along the *path to eternal life*, just as God always intended. Thus, the Eucharist is so much more than the manna that God provided as bodily sustenance for the Israelites (Exod 16). Ethicist John Kavanaugh tells us, "The Eucharist is about our salvation and our destiny, or it is nothing. It is the pledge of eternal forgiveness. And Communion is not mere bread for earthly flesh. Quite the contrary, it is nutrition for transformed bodies. It is the sustenance of wayfarers on their way beyond this life. It is the bread of angels, the food of heaven."[11]

Maintaining a Christlike presence in such a world is, however, a challenge that requires an alternative reality that moves beyond the lies and deceit of the human condition. Thus, the way Christians come together in the Eucharist and the way God chose to be present are important in reinforcing the presence of the kingdom of God. First, we participate in the liturgy of Eucharist not as individuals but as a united community. Cardinal Avery Dulles explains,

> Enacted in the power of the Holy Spirit, the sacrament unites the faithful to one another in the Church. This unitive capacity is symbolized by the elements themselves...bread is made up of grains gathered from hillsides and kneaded together in a single loaf; wine is produced from a multitude of grapes crushed in vats and commingled in a single cup. By participating in the mystery of Christ's body and blood, the Church is knit

together in a blessed communion of faith and love.[12]

This communion also forms one body of Christ in mystical union with the entire Communion of Saints throughout the ages. In addition, as one body, Christians recognize Christ in community with the dying, no matter how vulnerable, poor, or sick. It is in this community that Christians find renewed strength in sharing the good news.[13]

Second, Christ in the Eucharist continues to defy all the trappings of earthly power, prestige, and position. Instead, Christ is present as the most vulnerable are present. He comes in the fragile, insignificant, and common items of bread and wine. Cardinal Theodore McCarrick writes, "Would I want to be seen for the rest of time as a piece of bread that can be stepped on, broken, dishonored, and in a cup of wine that can be spilled out on the ground by someone who wants to make a point that they don't believe? Jesus is willing to do that....He doesn't care if this doesn't seem as glorious, magnificent or kingly as one would expect of God."[14] At the same time, nothing is more intimate than food and drink. A Christlike presence shares a similar kind of intimacy with the poor through the good news. To do so requires great humility on our part. Through Christ in the Eucharist, however, we see the humility of God that Christians accept within themselves.

Thus far I have attempted to reframe the Christian perspective on death and dying through a progressive unfolding of three key considerations. First, the secular culture's resistance to death influences Christians to deny the human condition and resist death instead of accepting death in light of Christ's life, death, and Resurrection. Instead Christians must become aware of the secular culture's misleading influences and reassess their life journeys in the light of Christ's truth. Second, lament is an important practice for expressing the difficulties of the human condition. The secular culture denies the need for lament, however, and instead focuses its faith and hope on human efforts. In contrast, Christians are called to awareness of the culture's wayward direction and to embrace lament focused on faith and hope in God. Third, in light of faith and hope in Christ's promises, Christians are called to the good news of dying to self through love of God and others. Christians are called to live their baptismal promise to "put on Christ" and celebrate Eucharist frequently in order to strengthen their call to live the good news.

Questions for Reflection

1. In what way does practicing self-giving acts of charity help mitigate the sting of bodily death?

2. Why does self-love seem to oppress people while love of God seems to bring freedom and peace? What practical examples do you find in the culture and in your own life experience that either support or refute this observation?

3. Reflect on the lessons of the wilderness school. Imagine that you are a student in this school. What questions or concerns would you raise to God about applying these lessons to your life?

4. Find one of your favorites among Jesus' parables. How does this parable demonstrate Christ's "living love," the "Galilee principle," Christ's vulnerability, his practice of the Beatitudes, and Christ's good news living? Next consider a parable (story) from your own life and reflect on those same five aspects. Describe the similarities and differences between them.

5. In receiving the Holy Eucharist, how do you find yourself living into Christ's alternative reality that transcends the lies and deceit of the human condition?

6. What effect does the Eucharist have on your desire to be a unifying presence to others no matter who they are?

CHAPTER FIVE

The Good News in the Trenches

Having attended to the culture's deceptions and denial of death and to theological resources for retrieving a Christian way of living and dying well, I now turn to the practical aspects of gleaning a perceived reality from clergy and church members concerning the key themes advanced in this book.[1] These themes are the basis for my inquiry into the following five areas: faith formation as it relates to the misdirected perspective of the secular culture concerning dying and death, the practice of lament within faith communities, living the good news as members of the body of Christ, the role of baptism and Eucharist in the faith community, and personal experiences of dying and death.

The first area of inquiry addresses the influence of the secular culture on the Christian understanding of dying and death with three key observations. First, formal faith formation programs that address cultural influences as well as the lifelong process of death and dying in the light of baptism and Christ's promises seem to be lacking. Most people live in two different worlds—that of Sunday and church and that of the day-to-day secular world—and the Church needs to embrace the task of helping people to connect these two worlds. This can be accomplished initially through the Sunday preaching and then reinforced through parish educational and formation programs. For example, one regular churchgoer who had often heard preachers talk about how to be a good Christian admitted that he never knew how to put this into practice until he got *pulled into* a care team that *showed him* how to use his gifts to help others. He now serves as a caregiver.

Second, churches seem to focus efforts on the needs of people at the physical end of life, especially the "last rites" and the funeral. Surprisingly, even grief support and bereavement seem to be addressed more through outside organizations than the Church itself. As one observer commented, "Much of the emphasis in local churches is on the funeral, the grieving process, and bereavement, not on preparing people for the inevitable fact that all of us must die." Thus many parish bereavement committees seem to focus chiefly on the immediate needs of the family during the funeral, providing food and domestic support,[2] while the long-term needs for grief support and bereavement are filled by local social agencies or hospital-affiliated services. Increasingly, funeral homes are extending their services for additional fees to include grief support and counseling. In some instances, the funeral homes are cooperating with the diocesan or district agencies and churches to provide their services within a religious context.

The third observation is that seminary training does not necessarily foster awareness of the effects of the culture in obfuscating the Christian meaning of dying. A former president of a Catholic seminary remarks that specific "work" to die rightly is usually not engaged until life is threatened. Many seminaries nowadays prepare seminarians for this work through a Clinical Pastoral Education (CPE) experience. At the same time, however, he believes that few Christian denominations or their seminaries actually require CPE for ordination. Duke Divinity School, for example, does not presently require CPE or even one pastoral care course for the Master of Divinity (MDiv) degree. In any case, even CPE does not address the lifelong work of connecting the meaning of dying through baptism with the daily dying of self through love of God and others.

The second area of inquiry speaks to the practice of lament and also provides three observations. First, few, if any, churches offer regularly scheduled communal services of lament. On occasion, some churches offer a healing service. On the level of lay pastoral support, a program called Stephen Ministry fosters a philosophy inclusive of a practice of lament because of the emphasis on "seeing God at work in and through us. God is the one who brings hope, love and forgiveness to hurting people."[3] Thus spiritual caregiver programs may offer an interpersonal component that supports lament.

The second observation concerning the practice of lament is that death seems to be a "dirty" word in many churches, just as it is in the Western secular culture. Thus, it is to be expected that if the secular culture denies the expression of emotion concerning the human condition, then many faith communities will follow suit.

One third and final observation on the practice of lament: Just as many churches lack an adequate pastoral presence to support the lifelong journey of dying and death as well as grief and loss support, congregations' limited acknowledgment of the need for lament seems to result in church members looking elsewhere for this type of support, such as secular support groups, therapists, and retreat centers. Visitors to one ecumenical retreat center, for example, admit that they come to this sacred space of sanctuary in order to lament in a safe place. The fact that 95 percent of the visitors to this retreat center are women raises the question on how, when, and where men meet their need to lament when framed within a secular culture that embraces "strong" men who don't show emotion.

The third area for inquiry provides three impressions of the present condition for members of the body of Christ in living the good news. First, inadequate support on the part of many congregations for the most vulnerable members on the perimeter of their faith communities does not emulate Jesus, who kept the least of all brethren at the core of his ministry. At best, "perimeter awareness" is a reactive rather than the proactive ministry that is the intent of living the good news. Typically a sick, dying, or homebound member must call and request a pastoral visit. Usually it is a single visit unless the member calls again to request another visit. Also, in my experience as a hospital chaplain, many pastors and ministers are limited in making hospital visits due to the many demands on their time, especially as fewer clergy serve bigger churches. In the worst situations, it seems that churches are able only to send the weekly bulletin to those members on the perimeter. One caregiver commented that receiving the weekly bulletin did little to support her and her mother's needs as full-time caregivers of her father. Their church had nothing in place "to keep them in the loop" once their active participation in church functions ceased during those difficult caregiving months. In addition, once caregivers get caught up in the difficult routines of care, they do not even notice that they are out of touch, yet they probably need to maintain church connections for their own sanity. Unless someone in the church *notices that a person, such as a caregiver, has needs*, then those needs remain unmet.

Just as is the case with grief and loss support, the secular world has found a way to fill this void with successful enterprises. For example, for-profit hospice centers are ubiquitous, while support organizations, such as A Helping Hand and Share the Care, are becoming commonplace.[4] On the other hand, some churches have extended their pastoral ministries through active parish and congregational nursing programs, lay ecclesial health care ministers, Stephen Ministers, and other outreach programs to the community and developing countries.

The second impression concerning living the good news as members of the body of Christ concerns support for vulnerable "perimeter" parishioners. As mentioned previously, one caregiver notes the lack of congregational support for her parents once they moved to their congregation's perimeter as care receiver and caregiver. However, another factor works against accepting the good news in self and others even in circumstances where it is offered. That is, the "American way" judges people's value to society based on their level of autonomy and independence as well as their ability to control their lives and destiny. Of course,

Christians know that such a system of judging a person's worth is the antithesis of the Gospel message. Yet this societal value system is ingrained into the thinking of church members both young and old. For instance, a caregiver's mother feels threatened with the idea of any type of outside help, even though she is tired and overwhelmed. A pastoral associate notes that many parishioners are desperately in need of help but refuse to ask. In many cases, people regard fellow church members as strangers who do not need to know their business or problems. Also, the "right to privacy" seems so ingrained in the American way of life that it precludes the acceptance of hospitality and kindness even when offered within faith communities. This division drives people into isolation and weakens the body of Christ.[5]

The third impression is that living the good news of dying to self and serving others is countercultural. Thus, it requires a prolonged effort within a well-connected faith community that models, teaches, trains, and supports both clergy and church lay parishioners on how to do this in everyday life. Many of the difficulties in fostering a long-term commitment to such an effort have already been mentioned, but they are worth summarizing again. First, the culture attempts to undermine Christian service efforts through abstraction and commodification of religious beliefs and practices for purposes of profit taking. Second, clergy are typically not trained in the ongoing "cradle to grave" practical application of theological doctrine and creedal beliefs. Third, the majority of good news role models are not elevated as examples but mostly remain hidden. Fourth, support for care programs for the average church attendee is both weak and sporadic. Five, caring for others through all life's passages is not modeled, taught, and reinforced appropriately. Unfortunately, few if any programs are available that "connect all these dots." Some of the resulting frustration is reflected in the comments of a director of a care support network who believes that one of his greatest challenges in gaining acceptance of his program is not necessarily with the church members but rather with the rigidity of church politics and its clergy. Because care support for the vulnerable is not typically viewed as a mainstay ministry such as music, youth, or education, whenever a pastor leaves a church any program that may be in place must again justify its value with the new pastor.

The role of baptism and the Eucharist in living the good news frames the fourth area of inquiry. This area contributes two worthwhile observations. First, baptism seems well understood as the sacrament of initiation into the Church as well as a gateway for forgiveness of sins. There are certainly various nuances concerning baptism depending on the faith tradition. However, the significance of dying to self and being born into a new life in Christ seems to escape most Christians in terms of the implications for daily living and acceptance of physical death. For example, one manual for the Catholic Rite of Christian Initiation of Adults (RCIA) includes scriptural reflections, explanations of the doctrine and the liturgy, but only one discussion question that hints at the challenges facing the new Christian for living the good news.[6] Two RCIA facilitators believe that the meaning of baptism as dying to self and all its implications are only touched on in RCIA.

As for children's faith formation, many programs seem to keep the focus upbeat and light with little or no mention of the implications of dying to self. However, most programs even for the youngest children are actively involving the children in service projects. Thus, although they do not explicitly connect these service opportunities with dying to self, the programs are modeling the Word in action.

The second observation is that, as with baptism, many Christians miss the significance of the Eucharist as unity with the People of God looking forward to what is not yet. This communion in unity with others is the food for the journey and the good news. Thus, infrequent communion actually deprives a Christian of the very food that nourishes the soul to live as Christ taught. "Very truly, I tell you, unless you eat the flesh of the Son of Man and drink his blood, you have no life in you" (John 6:53).

One pastor commented that in baptism, Christians are initiated into the priesthood of believers and are nourished in God's grace at the

Eucharist. This connection means helping people live out their faith both as givers and receivers. Another pastor expressed the mission of his parish in a similar way: "This parish is many things, but first of all it is a parish that finds its energy in the Eucharist. The parish takes the words St. Augustine used when inviting his people to communion. Holding high the body and blood of the Lord, Augustine would say, 'See what you are, and become what you see.' This faith community sees itself as the presence of Christ, broken and poured out for the world's salvation." An associate pastor regards the clergy as facilitators for helping the lay members become aware of their responsibility to connect with and support one another on a daily basis. Overall, both laypersons and clergy seem to agree that right now we do not always connect very well the meaning of baptism, the Gospel message, and the Eucharist to living in the secular world. The lens of the secular world has been quite successful in diffusing the meaning of baptism and Eucharist, thus detracting from the great joy of dying to self for love of God and others. On the other hand, the theological foundation for empowerment through baptism and Eucharist is already in place and being lived out through the active involvement of many church members in service. As a result, once better connection is made between the theology and the praxis already in place then dying to self and the sting of death should no more be feared and considered unmentionables.

The fifth area of inquiry provides three insightful threads of perspective about the personal experiences of death and dying. First, a person's response to dying and death both as a care receiver and caregiver appears to be influenced by the culture and its relation with the predominant religious traditions. In the West, the culture tends to abstract and commodify religious traditions for profit-taking purposes, while other cultures accept the religious tradition for what it is. For example, one person with whom I spoke, raised in the Zimbabwean culture, views death as an important part of life. This idea is taught at a young age as the young and old live together in families and villages. The young look after the old, sick, and dying, not as a chore but as a sacred and esteemed duty. When this woman's ninety-year-old mother was dying, family, friends, and parishioners surrounded her constantly. In addition, the clergy stopped by frequently as part of their daily rounds. Attending to and being present with the dying person are given the highest priority. Such an experience of dying recalls the tame death of the medieval *ars moriendi* tradition. In the West, care teams and hospices are slowly emerging as more popular ways of engaging the support of family and friends of the sick and dying; yet, most people still die in sterile healthcare settings that even limit the number of people who can attend to their sick or dying relative. Unfortunately, there is much at stake in regard to healthcare power and economics. There is little money to be made under the present reimbursement system when care is provided at home with friends and family in attendance.

In regard to the second insightful perspective, Western culture and society as well as mainline faith traditions do not appear to offer sufficient guidance on how to engage with old, disabled, sick, dying, and bereaved persons. Some potential caregivers steer clear of helping with sick or dying relatives because fear of not knowing what to do keeps them away. In one instance, a woman who had been taught by her sister-in-law to help care for a dying relative thereby not only overcame her fear and pitched in, but she also began support groups to help others find the courage to care for their loved ones.

The third and final insight is that some people seem to have a "calling" to caregiving, no matter what society or their faith communities do (or fail to do). For some persons, caring for family and friends is a longstanding family practice, even when it requires much patience and prayer. It is living the good news through the lens of the details of another person's life. In doing so, there is a definite dying to self. In addition, extending hospitality to older family members is a means of sharing daily life between generations. This confirms for the older generation the passing on of their story and creates extended story for the younger generations. As one caregiver says, "Little things count." She gives the example of her children watching her father-in-law take two hours to eat dinner while the family dog remains at attention for the entire time waiting for morsels of food to drop to the floor. In different circumstances, a cancer patient remembers how certain people signed on to her care team without hesitation. Finally, a caring couple invited a sick, elderly relative to live with them. This couple provides much food for thought in sharing the truth about their caregiving experience:

> It has to be a journey of the heart that requires prayer and daily devotion to God. Otherwise, it would be impossible and could destroy a marriage. You have to change your lifestyle; it requires sacrifice. There are different challenges every day. You never know what to expect when living with an older, sick relative. You must slow down as older people move slowly. It is a daily struggle for everyone. However, it can be a very rewarding experience. It takes so little to make them happy. For example, my grandpa likes his biscuits brown instead of light.

Questions for Reflection

1. How does the secular culture distract my attention from practicing my daily dying to self in light of the true meaning of my baptism?

2. What type of support does your church provide its members when they experience the death of a loved one? Does this support include an ongoing presence from bereavement through long-term grief?

3. When and how frequently is the practice of lament available at your church? Are all church members from children to the elderly invited to opportunities to practice lament on a routine basis? Reflect on your personal practice of lament. Does your practice of lament meet your daily needs and enrich your life journey?

4. How are the most vulnerable members of your church cared for on a regular basis? Are they found on the perimeter or in the center of your faith community? What program(s) exist "to notice the needs" of one another and then to respond accordingly?

5. In what ways does your church challenge the societal value system that judges people according to their level of autonomy, material success, and ability to take care of themselves?

6. What type of commitment has your faith tradition made to support a ministry of care support? Is the ministry of care support considered as essential as other ministries, such as worship, faith formation, youth, and finance? Describe briefly your vision of a ministry of care support for your faith community. What would it take to make this vision a reality? What effect would the reality of this vision have on your faith community?

7. How do the sacraments of baptism and Eucharist become the lived reality of Christ's body inviting your faith community to "see what you are and become what you see"?

8. In what ways are caregiving modeled and taught at your church and within your faith tradition? Describe your caregiver support network at your church. How do you monitor its effectiveness? Explain how the youth get involved in caregiving support of the vulnerable within your church.

CHAPTER SIX

Putting the Good News into Practice

This book has proposed that many Christians in the West have lost sight of the true meaning of death in light of Jesus Christ's death and Resurrection. Instead many Christians cling hopelessly to the secular culture's false promise of possible immortality. Despite the misleading direction of the culture, all is not lost.

In responding to this situation, I have attempted to reframe the Christian perspective on dying and death through a progressive unfolding of three important considerations. First, the secular culture's resistance to death influences Christians to deny the human condition and resist death instead of accept death in light of Christ's life, death, and Resurrection. Instead Christians must become aware of the secular culture's misleading influences and reassess their life journeys in the light of Christ's truth. Second, lament is an important practice for expressing the "bad news" or difficulties of the human condition. The secular culture denies the need for lament, however, and instead focuses faith and hope on human efforts. In contrast, Christians are called to awareness of the culture's wayward direction and to embrace lament focused on faith and hope in God. Third, in light of faith and hope in Christ's promises, Christians are called to the good news of dying to self through love of God and others. Christians are called to live their baptismal promise to "put on Christ" and celebrate the Eucharist frequently in order to strengthen their call to live the good news.

Once they acknowledge the bad news of the human condition and expressing lament in regard to this condition, Christians are then able to respond with hope to the good news: dying to self in baptism becomes a Christlike presence through love and service to others. The love flowing from the practice of the good news removes the sting of death.

Having awakened a new awareness of the culture's deceptions and denial of dying and death as well as having recouped related theological resources for a Christian practice for living and dying, I examined the reality of putting the major themes into practice. Clergy and laity of various Christian traditions identified certain shortcomings in faith formation touching on these areas. In general, faith formation does not appear either to provide adequate awareness of cultural deceit concerning dying and death or to foster a lifelong understanding of the true meaning of baptism as a dying to self in order to "put on Christ" and remove the sting of bodily death. As long as the sting of death remains then susceptibility to cultural deceit is high. Further, few opportunities exist for the routine practice of lament both as individuals and as a faith community. As long as the bad news of the human condition overlays the good news, then joyful lament in service to the most vulnerable is hidden on the perimeter of faith communities instead of becoming the central focus with Christ's life, death, and Resurrection.

I wish to conclude by offering the following ideas for revitalizing or renewing focus on a practice of daily living through daily dying as baptized Christians.

1. Faith Formation Programs

Faith formation programs, especially for teens and adults, need significant attention to building awareness of the ways and means of the secular culture in manipulating people to focus on consumption and all its trappings. This awareness could be reinforced—put into practice—by community action. Some appropriate programs include: Money & Faith; Manna and Mercy; Just Faith program; a church-wide book discussion of Vincent Miller's *Consuming Religion*; and a year-long guide for baptismal living such as Affirm! or other programs suggested by the North American Association for the Catechumenate (NAAC).[1]

2. The Practice of Lament

Faith communities may want to consider the importance of setting aside space and time for *reclaiming the practice of lament as a core practice of the faith community*. As we have attempted to show, until people openly acknowledge the bad news of the human condition, they will be less likely to live the good news. Here are two ideas for integrating lament into the faith community: First, a liturgy of lament is developed and adapted to a general lament service or monthly healing service that includes an anointing of the afflicted as well as a laying on of hands.[2] Second, lament services can also be scheduled for specific situations geared to the faith community as needs arise: for example, general bereavement, violent deaths, war, divorce, disabilities, and terminal illness. Lament prayer groups can also be organized through lay facilitation.

3. Relocation of the Most Vulnerable Members

Efforts should be made to relocate the most vulnerable members of the faith community to the center of the faith community. This requires that support programs be in place and running smoothly, once a needs assessment has been conducted to ascertain the types of support programs most appropriate for the faith community.

4. Evaluation of Seminary Training

On a broader scope, faith traditions may need to assess how well present-day seminary training prepares their clergy for leadership in living the good news. Most secular organizations are judged based on numbers (profits, sales, new members, value of assets, fundraising ability, and so on). How are seminary students encouraged to foster living the good news in a faith community rather than improve the numbers as a measure of their "success" and best practices? How does theological education prepare seminary students for discerning the effects and consequences of the death-denying culture (including the healthcare system) on the proper understanding of Christian death throughout life's passages? Does seminary training encourage limiting the function of healing to the ordained clergy? If so, support of the most vulnerable persons will be limited due to the many other ministerial tasks assigned to the clergy.

Finally, we return to the good news of the classic childhood bedtime prayer, remembering that Christ calls us as children of God to his one body in joyful lament through faith, hope, and love. So when "I lay me down to sleep," I have faith that the Lord has my soul in his keeping and I hope that the Lord will take my soul into his care "if I should die before I wake." And what about love? Because prayer is the lifting of our hearts and minds to God in an act of love, we join in love with God in the "so be it" or the "Amen." God's love is an eternal presence both in our living and dying. So if we die, "Amen." However, if we live for another day, then say "Amen" as well.

Notes

Introduction

1. This classic bedtime prayer for children (author unknown) originated in the eighteenth century. The longer version reads as follows:

> Matthew, Mark, Luke and John, bless the bed that I lie on.
> Before I lay me down to sleep, I give my soul to Christ to keep.
> Four corners to my bed, four angels there aspread,
> two to foot, and two to head, and two to carry me when I'm dead.
> I go to sea, I go to land, the Lord made me by his right hand.
> If any danger comes to me, sweet Jesus Christ, deliver me.
> He's the branch, and I'm the flower, pray God send me a happy hour.
> And if I die before I wake, I pray that Christ my soul will take.

2. Interestingly, most childhood infectious disease presents its worst symptoms in the evening and night. I speculate that before the time of antibiotics many children would succumb to infectious disease and its complications during the night.

3. This prayer reads as follows:

I thank You, Lord,
> for having been with me all this day.
> I thank You for the many good things
> You have done for me.

> I ask You to forgive me
> For anything I have done wrong.
> I know that You love me all the more
> if I am truly sorry.

> Bless my dear mother and father
> and my brothers and sisters,
> and all those who are kind to me.
> Help us all to love You more
> and serve You well tomorrow.
> Amen.

Lawrence Lovasik, SVD, *Saint Joseph Book of Prayers for Children* (Totowa, NJ: Catholic Book Publishing Company, 2000), 13.

4. The old Baltimore Catechism for elementary school children provides pictures of the "Way of the Cross" versus the "Way of Sin" reinforcing the message as to what "dying into Christ" (Rom 6:11) means in daily life. Thus, the Cross is real; sin and Satan are real; death

is real; and heaven and hell are real. [Confraternity of Christian Doctrine, *The Baltimore Catechism* (New York: Catholic Book Publishing Company, 1962)].

5. Human hope is a hope in human efforts that bonds past memory with the present while looking to the future. However, human hope leaves a gap between what is known in the present and the uncertainty of the future. On the other hand, hope in God (divine hope) is secure in God's future that is assured through Christ's death and Resurrection. "Let us hold fast the confession of our hope without wavering, for he who promised is faithful" (Heb 10:23). "The Holy Spirit....He poured upon us richly through Jesus Christ our Savior, so that we might be justified by his grace and become heirs in hope of eternal life" (Titus 3:6–7).

6. Eucharistic proclamation from the Eucharistic Prayer (Roman canon).

7. Episcopal Diocese of Washington, *Toward a Good Christian Death* (Harrisburg: Morehouse, 1999), 11–12.

8. To obtain the information I interviewed twenty persons who agreed to spend time talking with me for an hour or more. About half of these interviewees are Roman Catholic and the other half represents four other Christian traditions—Baptist, Methodist, Presbyterian, and Episcopalian. These interviews are not intended to represent any type of properly, randomized statistical sample and measurement tool but, rather, were informal discussions about their perspectives on formation within their faith communities and their experiences with dying and death in the model of Jesus Christ. Thus no universal conclusions can be drawn about or applied to the

actual situation concerning the dying and death experience of Christian traditions in the West.

Chapter One

1. Philippe Ariès, *Western Attitudes toward Death* (Baltimore: Johns Hopkins, 1974), 14.

2. Daniel Callahan, *The Troubled Dream of Life* (Washington: Georgetown, 2000), 30.

3. Ariès, 14.

4. Callahan, 30.

5. Ibid., 26.

6. Ibid.

7. Leo Tolstoy, *The Death of Ivan Ilyich* (New York: Random House, 1981), 86–87.

8. Immanuel Kant, *Foundations of the Metaphysics of Morals*, trans. Lewis White (New York: Macmillan, 1989), 85.

9. Joel Shuman, *The Body of Compassion* (Eugene: Wipf & Stock, 1999), 44.

10. Gerald McKenny, *To Relieve the Human Condition* (Albany: SUNY Press, 1997), 2.

11. Shuman, 15.

12. Geoffrey Wainwright, *For Us and Our Salvation* (Grand Rapids: Eerdmans, 1997), 18.

13. Alastair MacIntyre, "Medicine Aimed at the Care of Persons," in *Philosophical Medical Ethics: Its Nature and Significance*, editors S. Spicker and H. Engelhardt (Dordrecht: Reidel, 1977), 89.

14. Nancy Gibbs and Amanda Bower, "Q: What Scares Doctors? A: Being the Patient," *Time* (May 1, 2006): 42–51.

15. Ibid., 52.

16. Nicholas Lash, *A Matter of Hope: A Theologian's Reflections on the Thought of Karl Marx* (Notre Dame: Notre Dame Press, 1982), 72; quoted in Joel Shuman and Keith Meador, *Heal Thyself* (New York: Oxford, 2003), 83.

17. Shuman, 45.

18. McKenny, 20.

19. Allen Verhey, *Reading the Bible in the Strange World of Medicine* (Grand Rapids: Eerdmans, 2003), 71.

20. Tolstoy, 87.

21. Wendell Berry, *Hannah Coulter* (Kentucky: Shoemaker & Hoard, 2004), 160–161.

22. *Ars moriendi* ("art of dying") is theological literature that emerged in the fifteenth century to prepare both Protestant and Catholic persons for the task of dying. This literature recognized that dying is an art and a learned behavior that a person does either well or poorly. Vogt identifies three virtues that seem crucial in this learning process. These are patience, compassion, and hope. C. Vogt, *Patience, Compassion, Hope, and the Christian Hope of Dying Well* (Lanham: Rowman & Littlefield, 2004), 2.

23. Callahan, 26.

24. Thomas à Kempis, *The Inner Life*, trans. Leo Sherley-Price (New York: Penguin, 1952), 34. Also, http://www.leaderu.com/cyber/books/imitation/imitation.html.

25. Philippe Ariès, *The Hour of Our Death*, trans. H. Weaver (New York: Knopf, 1981), 559 and 603.

26. Romans 5:19–21.

27. Pope John Paul II, "Discourse of John Paul II to the Participants of the Working Group," in *Working*

Group on the Determination of Brain Death and Its Relationship to Human Death (December 10–14, 1989) (Pontificiae Academiae Scientiarum Scripta Varia, 83), eds. R. J. White, H. Angstwurm, and I. Carrasco de Paula (Vatican City: Pontifical Academy of Sciences, 1992), no. 2, p. xxiv; quoted in William E. May, *Catholic Bioethics and the Gift of Human Life* (Huntington: Our Sunday Visitor, 2000), 287.

28. Paul Crowley, SJ, *Unwanted Wisdom* (New York: Continuum, 2005), 131.

29. United States Catholic Conference, *Catechism of the Catholic Church* (New York: Doubleday, 1994), 285.

30. Cardinal Avery Dulles, "The Eucharist, Source and Summit of Ecclesial Life," *Magnificat* (October 2005): 6.

31. Dorothee Sölle, *Suffering* (Philadelphia: Fortress, 1975), 157.

32. D. Anthony Storm, "Commentary on 'The Sickness Unto Death,'" n.p. http://sorenkierkegaard.org/kw19.htm.

33. St. Augustine, *The Confessions*, trans. Maria Boulding, OSB (New York: Random House, 1998), 59, 61.

34. General Convention of the Episcopal Church, *Faithful Living, Faithful Dying* (Harrisburg: Morehouse, 2000), 10.

Chapter Two

1. Allen Verhey, *Reading the Bible in the Strange World of Medicine* (Grand Rapids: Eerdmans, 2003), 124–125.

2. Mary Catherine Hilkert, "Edward Schille-beeckx: Encountering God in a Secular and Suffering World," *Theology Today* (October 2005): 381.

3. That is, *kenosis* as self-emptying similar to what Paul described about Christ in the hymn of Philippians 2:5–11.

4. A dirge contrasts past glories and present misery (A. Verhey, 124). Many scholars do not consider Lamentations a dirge because of the glimmer of hope in looking to God provided in the center of the book (Lam 3:21–33).

5. Claus Westermann, *The Living Psalms* (Grand Rapids: Eerdmans, 1984), 74.

6. David Rensberger, *HarperCollins Study Bible* (New York: HarperCollins, 1989), 2035.

7. Jesus' hope in his Father seems paradoxical in that he suffers distance from the Father yet places his trust in the Father's presence.

8. Christopher Vogt, *Patience, Compassion, Hope, and the Christian Art of Dying Well* (Lanham: Rowman, 2004), 109.

Chapter Three

1. As sacraments, both baptism and Eucharist use common ordinary occurrences or substances as symbols that point beyond themselves to the loving presence of Jesus. That is, baptism's symbols are the *darkness* of the tomb and the raising to the *light* of Christ through *water*. Eucharist's symbols are *bread* and *wine*.

2. Bert Ghezzi, "Significance of the Sign of the Cross," pg.1 [cited 14 May, 2006]. Online: http://www.

ewtn.com/library/Liturgy/ZSIGNCRO>HTM.

3. Don Saliers, *Worship as Theology* (Nashville: Abingdon, 1994), 57.

4. In baptism, as in all sacraments, God's assured presence, the Christian's witness to God's presence, and God's eschatological dimension exist within the sacrament's rite.

5. United States Catholic Conference, *Catechism of the Catholic Church* (New York: Doubleday, 1994), 368.

6. Saliers, 60.

7. Ibid., 61.

8. Ibid., 26.

9. *Catechism of the Catholic Church*, 377.

10. Peter De Vries, *The Blood of the Lamb* (Chicago: University of Chicago, 1961).

11. Ibid., 180.

12. Ibid., 182, 208.

13. Ibid., 206.

14. Ibid., 212.

15. Ibid.

16. Ibid.

17. Ibid., 218–221.

18. Ibid., 223.

19. Ibid., 228.

20. Ibid., 236.

21. Ibid., 234. Cf. the book of Numbers 6:24–26.

22. Ibid.

23. Ibid., 237.

24. Ibid., 246.

25. Nicholas Wolterstorff, *Lament for a Son* (Grand Rapids: Eerdmans, 1987).

26. Ibid., 49.

27. Ibid., 50.
28. Ibid., 51.
29. Ibid., 65.
30. Ibid., 70.
31. Ibid., 83.
32. Ibid., 85.
33. Ibid., 92-93.
34. Tolstoy, 33.
35. Ibid., 77.
36. Ibid., 111.
37. Berry, 50–51 and 80.
38. Ibid., 161.
39. Ibid.

Chapter Four

1. Jürgen Moltmann, "Resurrection as Hope," *Harvard Theological Review* 61 (1968): 143 in J. Shuman, 83.

2. Augustine quoted without reference in Joel Shuman's *The Body of Compassion*, 95.

3. Daniel Erlander, *Manna and Mercy: A Brief History of God's Unfolding Promise to Mend the Entire Universe* (Mercer Island: The Order of Saints Martin and Teresa, 1992), 6–15. Daniel Erlander, P.O. Box 1059, Freeland, WA 98249.

4. Ibid., 9.

5. Henri Nouwen, *Our Greatest Gift* (New York: HarperCollins, 1994), 109.

6. Erlander, 44–45.

7. This is Roberto Goizueta's explanation in "From Calvary to Galilee," *America* (April 17, 2006): 14.

8. Dietrich Bonhoeffer, *Meditations on the Cross* (Louisville: Westminster, 1996), 80–81.

9. Nouwen, 26.

10. John Zizioulas, *Being as Communion* (Crestwood: St.Vladimir's, 1993), 55–56 in Joel Shuman, *The Body of Compassion*, 107.

11. John Kavanaugh, SJ, "Eternal Sustenance," *Daybreaks* (2006):55.

12. Cardinal Avery Dulles, SJ, "The Eucharist, Source and Summit of Ecclesial Life," *Magnificat* (October 2005): 8.

13. *Catechism of the Catholic Church*, 391.

14. Cardinal Theodore McCarrick, "The Strength Is in the Miracle," *Dialog* (November 11, 2005): 9.

Chapter Five

1. The information in this section is based on interviews with twenty persons. It is thus anecdotal rather than scientific, although the interviewees represent a cross section of ordained and lay ministers in different Christian denominations as well as other participants in or receivers of church-based ministry.

2. One such effective ministry in widespread use in Catholic parishes is the Ministry of Consolation.

3. Stephen Ministry is a program that selects, trains, and supervises lay church members to provide one-to-one Christian care to persons in need on behalf of their faith community. According to their Web site, "Stephen Ministers typically are assigned one care receiver at a time and meet with that person one hour each week. Stephen Ministers usually serve for two

years, which includes an initial fifty hours of training followed by twice monthly supervision and continuing education sessions." (www.stephenministries.org)

4. A Helping Hand is a nonprofit organization in North Carolina that serves senior citizens and people temporarily and permanently disabled by fostering wellness, dignity, and independence at all stages of life. Share the Care is a nonprofit organization dedicated to educating the public, health professionals, and clergy about group caregiving as a proven option for meeting the needs of the seriously ill, the dying, those in rehabilitation, the elderly in need of caregiving, and their caregivers.

5. As a former secular marketing expert, I can confirm that isolation and division of people as target consumers are the strategies for selling products and services in a capitalistic society. "Divide and conquer" is a key concept because isolation is contrary to the human being's social nature. When isolated the human being becomes easily manipulated by cognitive psychological methods used to sell products and services.

6. Mark Link, SJ, *The Catholic Vision* (Allen: Tabor, 1989), #19.

Chapter Six

1. Jan Sullivan Dockter, *Money and Faith Study Circle Handbook* (Ministry of Money, 2001), *Manna and Mercy*, see Chapter 4, n. 3; www.ministryofmoney.org; Just Faith, www.justfaith.org; Vincent Miller, *Consuming Religion: Christian Faith and Practice in a Consumer Culture* (New York: Continuum, 2005); www.catechumenate.org.

2. In the Roman Catholic tradition, the sacrament of anointing of the sick fills this need. A good example of a nonsacramental Liturgy of Lament is one that Richard Rohr, OFM, uses at the Center for Action and Contemplation and is available at http://www.cacradicalgrace.org.

For Further Reading

Aging with Dignity. *Five Wishes*. Tallahassee: Aging with Dignity, 2005.

Ariès, Philippe. *The Hour of Our Death*. Translated by H. Weaver. New York: Knopf, 1981.

———. *Western Attitudes toward Death*. Baltimore: Johns Hopkins, 1974.

Berry, Wendell. *Hannah Coulter*. Kentucky: Shoemaker & Hoard, 2004.

Bonhoeffer, Dietrich. *Meditations on the Cross*. Translated by Douglas Stott. Louisville: Westminster, 1996.

Browning, Don. *A Fundamental Practical Theology*. Minneapolis: Fortress, 1991.

Callahan, Daniel. *The Troubled Dream of Life*. Washington: Georgetown, 2000.

Capossela, Cappy, and Sheila Warnock. *Share the Care*. New York: Fireside, 2004.

Cashman, Kevin. *Ministry of Money*. http://ministryofmoney.org.

Center for Action and Contemplation. "Liturgy of Lament Template." http://cacradicalgrace.org.

Crowley, Paul, SJ. *Unwanted Wisdom*. New York: Continuum, 2005.

De Vries, Peter. *The Blood of the Lamb*. Chicago: University of Chicago, 1961.

Dulles, Cardinal Avery. "The Eucharist, Source and Summit of Ecclesial Life." *Magnificat* (October 2005): 6.

Episcopal Diocese of Washington. *Toward a Good Christian Death*. Harrisburg: Morehouse, 1999.

Erlander, Daniel. *Manna and Mercy*. Mercer Island: Order of Saints Martin and Teresa, 1992.

Farley, Edward. *Theologia—The Fragmentation and the Unity of Theological Education*. Eugene: Wipf & Stock, 2001.

General Convention of the Episcopal Church. *Faithful Living, Faithful Dying*. Harrisburg: Morehouse, 2000.

Gibbs, Nancy, and Amanda Bower. "Q: What Scares Doctors? A: Being the Patient." *Time* (May 1, 2006): 42–51.

Goizueta, Roberto. "From Calvary to Galilee." *America* (April 17, 2006): 14.

Hilkert, Mary Catherine. "Edward Schillebeeckx: Encountering God in a Secular and Suffering World." *Theology Today* (October 2005): 381.

Kavanaugh, John. "Eternal Sustenance." *Daybreaks* (2006): 55.

MacIntyre, Alastair. "Medicine Aimed at the Care of Persons." In *Philosophical Medical Ethics: Its*

Nature and Significance, ed. S. Spicker and H. Engelhardt, 89. Dordrecht: Reidel, 1977.

McCarrick, Cardinal Theodore. "The Strength Is in the Miracle." *Dialog* (November 11, 2005): 9.

McKenny, Gerald. *To Relieve the Human Condition.* Albany: SUNY Press, 1997.

Miller, Vincent. *Consuming Religion: Christian Faith and Practice in a Consumer Culture.* New York: Continuum, 2005.

Moltmann, Jürgen. "Resurrection as Hope." *Harvard Theological Review* 61 (1968): 143.

National Hospice and Palliative Care Organization. *Caring Connections.* Alexandria: NHPCO, 2005.

North American Association for the Catechumenate (NAAC). "Resources and Practical Help." http://www.catechumenate.org/section_9_detail.cfm?sid=9&cid=3.

Nouwen, Henri. *Our Greatest Gift.* New York: HarperCollins, 1994.

Roberts, Gina. "Consumerism: A False Path in the Search for Soul." *The Independent* (June 2006): n.p.

Seasons of the Spirit. "Bringing Faith to Life." http://www.spiritseasons.com/sublevel.taf?site_uid1=11496&hallway_uid1.

Shuman, Joel. *The Body of Compassion.* Eugene: Wipf & Stock, 1999.

————. and Keith Meador. *Heal Thyself.* New York: Oxford, 2003.

Sölle, Dorothee. *Suffering*. Philadelphia: Fortress, 1975.

Tolstoy, Leo. *The Death of Ivan Ilyich*. New York: Random House, 1981.

Verhey, Allen. *Reading the Bible in the Strange World of Medicine*. Grand Rapids: Eerdmans, 2003.

Vogt, Christopher. *Patience, Compassion, Hope, and the Christian Art of Dying Well*. Lanham: Rowman & Littlefield, 2004.

Wainwright, Geoffrey. *For Us and Our Salvation*. Grand Rapids: Eerdmans, 1997.

Westermann, Claus. *The Living Psalms*. Grand Rapids: Eerdmans, 1984.

Wilson, Kevin. "What Is Stephen Ministry All About?" http://stephenministries.org.

Wolterstorff, Nicholas. *Lament for a Son*. Grand Rapids: Eerdmans, 1987.

Zizioulas, John. *Being as Communion*. Crestwood: St. Vladimir's, 1993.

ILLUMINATIONBOOKS

Other Books in the Series